Table of Contents

Important Video Links and Contacts	5
INTRODUCTION	6
Multiple sources or income	8
Pursuing My Passion	9
A Vision	10
ONLINE JOB SITES	12
Upwork	13
Freelancer	15
Guru	15
Navigating The Job Sites	16
How the Websites Earn From You	16
Signing Up	16
Nature of Work	18
Academia research	22
Craigslist	24
Thumbtack	26
LinkedIn	27
TIPS ON HOW TO FIND WORK	29
Step 1: Create Your Online Profile	30
Platform-based Profile	30
PDF Version Of Your Profile	37
Personal Website	39

Other Tips	50
Step 2: Writing a Resume or Portfolio	52
The Unique Selling Proposition	52
For Fresh Graduates	54
Your Professional Experience	55
For Fresh Graduates	57
Resume Examples	59
Step 3: Applying for Jobs	61
First Goal: Accumulate reviews	61
How to Secure Jobs ASAP	61
Writing an Application Letter	64
Your Online Visibility	67
Step 4: Grow	83
Branch out and set up a company	83
Scout for Clients on Social Media	84
CHALLENGES ENCOUNTERED	85
Starting Out	85
Clients Not Paying	86
Time Zones	86
Internet Speed	87
USEFUL RESOURCES	88
CHECKLIST	97

This page was intentionally left blank.

This page was intentionally left blank.

Important Video Links and Contacts

If you have questions, concerns or clarifications, please email f@asianeac.com or message me directly on any of my social media channels:

- YouTube
- Instagram
- Twitter

Thank you,

INTRODUCTION

NOTE: This is a personal story and you may skip to ONLINE JOB SITES CHAPTER to get to the meat.

In the 10 years I did online work-from-home jobs with clients coming from seven different online freelance job sites, I earned more than $230,000.00. Below is a screenshot of my earnings from one of the job sites, Upwork. This does not include the money that I earned from clients that my existing online client referred to me with which I conducted business outside of the online job sites.

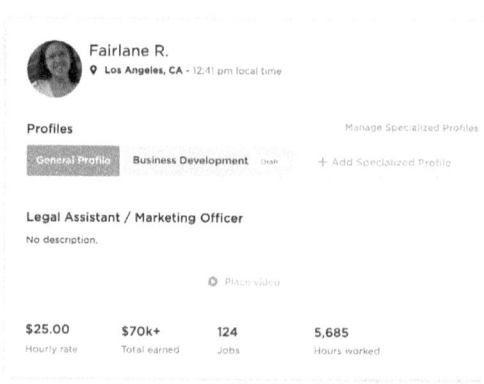

Considering I worked an average of 2 hours everyday because I had a full-time job and I was writing scripts on the side, it wasn't that bad. From that money, I bought a house, something my family and I never had growing up and paid for my niece's education. I am not bragging but I am very proud of what I have accomplished and all it took was time and patience in establishing myself online.

My dad, my mom, my sister and I lived in a small room in my grandmother's house. There were 3 other families there. There were 29 people sharing one bathroom. It was my biggest motivation to be able to buy a house. I knew I needed to work an extra job but it wouldn't pay much. It will take me forever to afford a house. I needed a higher paying job and online work will allow me to do that. Minimum wage is a tenth of US workers. That was the way to go.

Through the years, it has proven to be the most consistent source of work. Clients recommended me to their friends and family. Eventually, I had to create an agency. I managed a team of 10, from developers to writers, to accommodate the workload. I have since moved to the U.S. which only made my portfolio thicker and I attracted more clients. I'll discuss that in depth later.

Multiple sources or income

I already had a full-time job. I was working as an account manager for one of the biggest advertising agencies in the world, DDB worldwide. I was also writing scripts for one of the biggest production companies in the Philippines, Regal films. Below is a screenshot of my

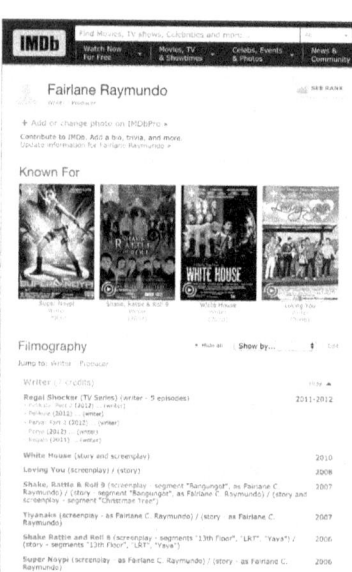

IMDB Profile. However, I always believed that I needed multiple sources of income. The most successful businessmen diversify and their bank accounts are a million times thicker than mine.

Losing a job was not an option for me. I was the breadwinner

in the family. I was financing the education of my niece. My father also went through two strokes and the Philippines didn't have a good health program. I also wanted to provide my family better experiences, especially my niece who I consider my firstborn.

Pursuing My Passion

Although I was enjoying my work in the advertising agency, it wasn't my first love and it's not my passion. I love writing. It is not a very lucrative job in the Philippines. Unless you become one of the top writers. I did not have the luxury of spending years to establish myself as a writer. I needed to earn money as soon as I graduated from college. I could not continue burdening my family with my own finances. I simply had to find a way to pursue my passion and still earn.

A Vision

More importantly I had a vision for myself. I knew that I did not want to work an 8 to 5 job forever. I know the time will come when I want to travel and do other things. I needed to have a source of income that would allow me the flexibility to travel and pursue my other passions. The first couple of years, I had to establish myself. Just like any other professional starting in a new industry, I was underpaid. I didn't mind at that time because I had a full-time job.

I considered it an investment I had to make if I ever wanted to reach a point in my life when I can do what I love doing and not worry about the bills getting paid.

In retrospect, the best thing I did was start when I felt like doing it. My first online source of work is Upwork. Once I got familiar with the industry, I started branching out to other online work sources. At the time, I was still living in the Philippines but all of my clients were in the United States, Australia and Europe.

Eventually, I started signing up on other freelance work websites like Freelancer, Prospect solution, and Academia-Research. After I got a little bit more established, other websites started becoming a source of work including LinkedIn, Facebook, my own website and specialized job sites.

ONLINE JOB SITES

Here are the job sites I used to get online work:

- Upwork: http://www.upwork.com/
- Academia-Research: https://www.academia-research.com/
- Freelancer: https://www.freelancer.com/
- Guru: https://www.guru.com/
- Thumbtack: https://www.thumbtack.com/
- LinkedIn: https://www.linkedin.com/
- Facebook: http://www.facebook.com
- Personal Website: http://www.madsoulasylum.com
- Specialized Job Sites
    - Baby Sitting: http://www.care.com/
    - Rover: https://www.rover.com/

Now let's go through each of the websites and discuss what field each website specializes in, if any, advantages and disadvantages, and other things you need to know before you sign up. I will first discuss Upwork, Freelancer, and Guru. They all offer the same basic features.

Upwork

Charges
- You can apply or bid for up to 10 jobs/projects for free. If you want to be able to apply for up to $100 jobs or projects, you need to pay $20 per month.
- You get charged 10% of your total fee.

Why sign up in Upwork

UpWork is the most prolific in terms of job posts, quality of employers, and layout. This is where I started as a freelancer, grew and eventually established my own company. I also used Elance but several years ago, Upwork (still Odesk then), bought Elance.

Their job categories include marketing, writing, directing, voice-over talents, Legal Services, project management, clerical jobs, research and others.

This is where I would suggest you start.

Freelancer

Charges

- Fee for fixed price projects is 10% or $5.00 USD, whichever is greater, and 10% for hourly projects. They may charge for certain services but those are optional.
- Like Upwork, you can get more bids monthly if you upgrade your account. To start, you get 6 free bids for free.

Why sign up in Freelance

Freelancer has been around the longest. It is still a good site but I personally find the layout disorganized and not the most friendly in terms of usability but if you can get around it, it has just as many job posts as Upwork.

The quality of employers is just as good but there is also more competition. So, while the jobs are just good, starting here may be a bit challenging.

Guru

Charges
- Depending on your membership level, Guru may charge between 5-9%.
- There are 5 membership levels, Free, Basic ($11.95mo), Professional ($21.95mo), Business ($33.95mo), $4 to Executive.

Why sign up in Guru

Since it is the least popular of the three, you will also have less competition. However, that would also mean less opportunity. There are more Middle Eastern employers here.

The layout of the site is just as friendly as Upwork.

Navigating The Job Sites

How the Websites Earn From You

There are several ways the job site earns from you:
- They get a percentage of your earnings,
- All of them have a free membership tier but they limit the number of applications or bids you can send. If you want to bid for more projects, you will have to pay for membership,
- Some of these sites also offer "certifications" and "priority bids".

Signing Up

<u>Create an online profile</u>. The first step is to create an online profile or online resume that will be visible to the employer. I am going to go through the step by step procedure on how to do this and tips on how to make it attractive to employers.

Free or paid. A free account will get you anywhere between five to ten bids per month. If you want to send more, you may have to pay anywhere between $10 a month to $50. A paid account also has other benefits such as seeing the bids of other Freelancers and it can automatically get you on top of the list when an employer checks the bids. On the next page are screencaps of the membership freelancer sites.

Proving your identity. In all of these websites, you need to provide a valid identification. This has been a source of great discomfort for a lot of people but do remember that these are legitimate jobs. Just like any other employer, you would want to know the identity of the person you are working with. If you are a freelancer from the United States of America or Canada, you need to provide your tax identification or social security number.

Getting Paid. When you get paid depends on the job type you get. For project-based work, you can either set certain milestones or get paid after the project. For, hourly jobs, you get paid once a week and the exact day differs from website to website.

You can link your credit card, bank account, PayPal or Payoneer account. You get paid on your local currency.

Nature of Work

As mentioned above, there are two types of projects or works on upwork:

- Project basis
- Per hour work

The per hour work allows you to automatically get paid at the end of the week provided the employer does not contest your hours. You will need to install the website's time tracking application. This allows you to log in when you start working and takes a screenshot of your screen every several minutes. This will then become visible to the employer at the end of the work week. The employer gets several days to review the screenshots. The employer can review the timesheet. They are given several days to review and contest but Upwork, Freelancer, and Guru advise that if there is any conflict, the employer and the employee resolve it by themselves first but if the employer and the employee are unable to get to a resolution, then Upwork can do a mediation.

    The Per Project work gets you paid per milestone or at the end of the project, depending on what you agree with the employer. The websites will actually hold the total cost of the entire project and will only release it once the employer approves your final output. It does not guarantee that you are going to get paid. If the employer contests your work hours or quality of work, you may try to settle it directly or bring to mediation. If the mediation sides with you then you get paid. However, the website holding the money guarantees that the employer has enough money on its account to pay you if the project finishes successfully.

Upwork Membership Plans

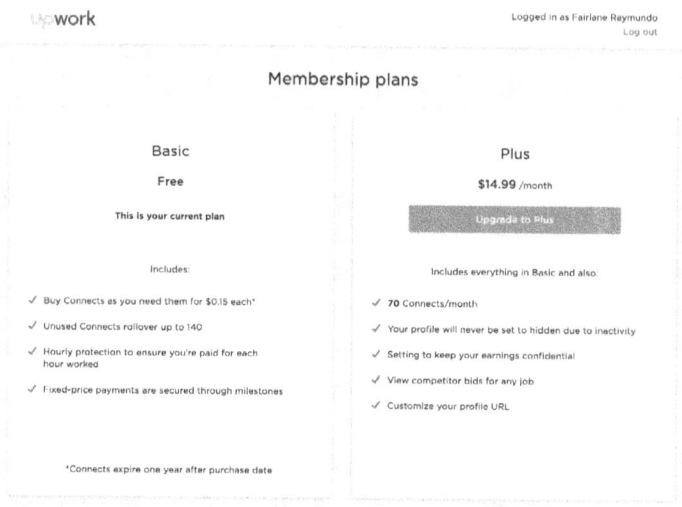

Guru Membership Plans

	Basic	Basic+	Professional	Business	Executive
	Free	$8.95	$15.95	$24.95	$39.95
Project Fee	8.95%	8.95%	6.95%	5.95%	4.95%
Total Bids	10 bids	600 bids / 50	600 bids / 50	600 bids / 50	600 bids / 50
Skill tests	$4.95	$2.95	FREE	FREE	FREE
Earnings boost in search		$1,000	$2,000	$4,000	$8,000
Bids Rollover			✓ Limit 100	✓ Limit 200	✓ Limit 300
Submit Premium Proposals			✓ Cost 5 bids	✓ Cost 4 bids	✓ Cost 3 bids

Freelancer Membership Plans

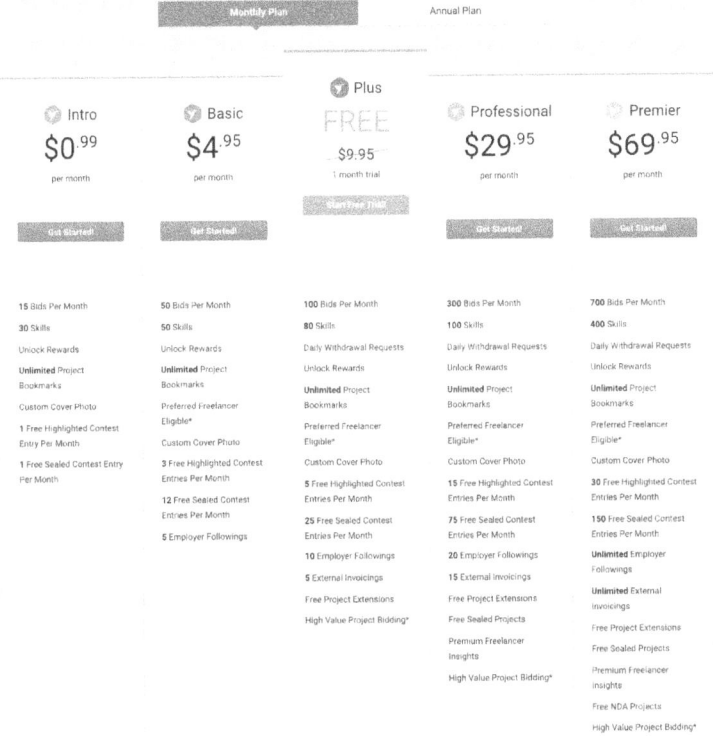

Academia research

Academia Research is geared towards academic research. Most of the customers or clients are students. They require high quality, well-researched with proper formatting and citations. Some of the jobs are actual "research requirements" for thesis, doctorate, and term papers for different academic purposes.

Unlike the three previous websites, jobs in Academia Research are almost always per project basis. You do not get paid until after the work is done or after certain milestones which you should negotiate prior to taking the project.

It is, however, highly lucrative. I used to do research for a thesis paper per month and my bills for the entire month would be fully paid. I know many of you would doubt I can finish a thesis paper in a month but I did it and did so while I was doing other works for other sites. Yes, many of them came back to me offering a bonus after they get an A.

It gave me a chance to read about different topics and I have always liked reading and learning.

When you're new, you will be given simple jobs like a reaction paper or simple baby thesis proposal. But as you establish your credibility, the better the jobs you may be able to get.

Academia Research is primarily for researchers or writers but if you are a specialist in different Industries you are most likely going to have high paying projects as long as your specialization fits a job requirement. For example, if you're an engineer and you can write. You can get jobs for academic articles about engineering. If you're a nurse, there are a lot of papers that require research and writing about biology and other things.

> **Hot Tip!**
>
> I know that many of you don't like writing even though you have the expertise. There's an easy solution. You can hire a writer to polish your thoughts into writing. You can record yourself narrating your ideas and then pass it on to someone to put it into writing. You can split the payment but you can hire a lot of writers on other job sites that will more than fit your budget.

Craigslist

Craigslist is mostly geared towards US-based freelancers. It is good for clerical and part-time work. If you want to earn extra money during the weekend, you can easily find a weekend receptionist job in some Spa, or teach languages online.

When I was new in the U.S., Craigslist is one of the two job sites that I tried. I didn't have a lot of luck finding full-time jobs there. I found plenty of part-time work, most of which were clerical or manual work. Since I was new in the US, I wanted and needed as much work as I could get. Aside from the full-time job that I had, I decided to do lots of part-time work to establish my network. I was still active in Upwork but since those were work from home jobs, I needed to build my physical Network.

One of the jobs that I got that turned out to be one of the best ones based on my objectives. I worked as a receptionist for a spa during the weekend. Many full-time employees prefer to work only during the weekdays. Hospitality businesses have their best days on the weekends. I was the perfect employee for them. No one was threatened with my presence since it was clear to them it was not a career I wanted to pursue and that also made me "easier" when it comes to following procedures and rules. I wasn't really there to move up the ranks,

My friend also got constant waiting jobs through Craigslist. For a time, I also became a personal online assistant for a music producer, and I was handling most of his scheduling, follow-ups on invoices, sending out newsletters, and posting social media content. I like that job but time came when he actually needed somebody that would be reporting to his studio on a regular basis, and it was not something that I wanted to do so I had to let it go.

Thumbtack

Thumbtack is no different from Upwork. People post their projects on the site and you can bid but unlike Upwork, Thumbtack also features jobs that require you to meet the client physically such as Plumbing, construction work, photography, and others.

That's why Thumbtack usually pairs you with jobs that are close to you if the job requires you to physically go to the client.

The biggest disadvantage may be the communications cost. Whenever an employer communicates with you and you want to respond, you will be charged a certain amount per response.

LinkedIn

LinkedIn is a social network for professionals. However, once you establish your presence and if you have a well-written profile, you have a good chance of being approached by employers. Employers actually use LinkedIn to find people to fill their employment requirements.

I actually found a job for a very successful YouTuber through LinkedIn. It was him who inspired me to open my own channel.

The best part is that it's free to be in LinkedIn. You can pay for membership that will give you privileges such as seeing who visited your profile but I personally never paid for membership and have no problem looking for work or getting spotted by Headhunters. Below I will be sharing some more tips on how you can utilize LinkedIn to grow your network and increase your chances of connecting to possible employers.

  There have been other online freelance websites but I have never really tested them because I don't need them as of the moment. I already have a full-time job, a sall business and my own YouTube channel, Twitter account, and Patreon. I would probably go back to Upwork or Freelancer to get new clients rather than try new websites. Some of my cousins and friends are still in Upwork and Freelancer.

TIPS ON HOW TO FIND WORK

Step 1: Create Your Online Profile

Opening accounts and setting up your online profile Is no different from creating or writing your own resume. You need to put your job history skills and qualifications but the devil is always in the details.

Platform-based Profile

Each of the websites mentioned allows you to create a platform-based profile. Some sites will allow you to create your resume in their system or upload a pdf version of your resume.

Photos are usually optional but you need to prove your identity by sending a scanned copy of a government-issued IDs and using your legal name. You do have to remember that you're dealing with actual employers that are willing to pay for your work. Although it is online, it is no different from working for an employer. Employers on these websites want to know who is working for them. That is also why most freelancers opt to put a photo on their profile page. It helps prove your authenticity.

It is also important to make your online profile as complete as possible because these websites have algorithms that crawl your profile to determine if you match the requirements of possible employees.

Benefits of a platform-based profile

I would recommend doing an online profile instead of uploading a document because of the following reasons:
- It's easier for the website to crawl your qualifications and match you to employers or project requirements
- You can pack as many experiences, certifications and other qualifications
- You can use links to direct employers to an online portfolio or samples of your work visible online

Things You Will Need To Create An Online Profile

Make sure you have the following:
- Payment methods (where your payments will be sent):
    - Paypal
    - Bank Accounts
    - Credit Card
- Government issued ID
- Social Security Number (for residents of the U.S.)
- Pdf version of your portfolio of work samples
- Word version of your resume to copy and paste on the website's profile
- Professional looking photo

Tips When Creating a Platform-based Profile

A. Be Concrete

One of the worst mistakes applicants make when writing their own resume is using general terms or as we call it in advertising "motherhood statements". Provide tangible evidence of your claims instead of simply making a claim.

Providing concrete evidence immediately gives the prospective employer a concrete idea of how you fit the requirement. Further, you gain the edge of being more memorable instead of being one of the many who simply claim to be an expert on the field they happen to need.

See examples below:

✗	✓
expert on WordPress	created over 50 websites using Wordpress platform varying from corporate website online magazines online store
proficient in C++	worked for 4 software companies developing wi used programs like Adobe several white hacking too

B. Use Relevant Keywords

Learn what are the most searched keywords by employers when looking to fill positions and use those terms on your online profile. For example, if they are specific about the software programs they use and you actually know how to use those, put the names of those software on your profile.

The question is where do you find keywords?

To be honest, I often just use my own gut feel on what to put on my own profile. However there are different websites you can use to see what words related to your industry are most often searched.

Google ads. You can create an account and actually navigate the back end for you to search for keywords without actually having to pay.

Step 1: Enter the keyword on the search bar and click Search.

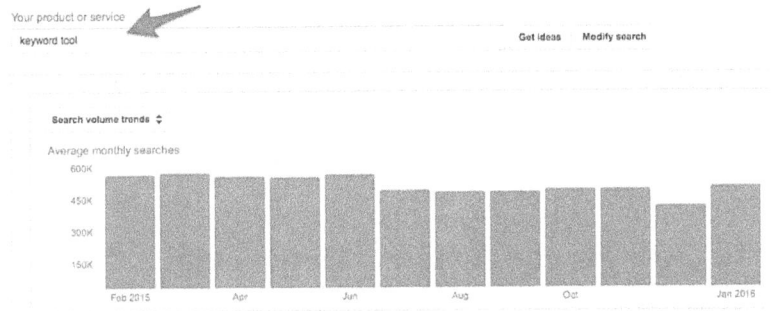

Step 2: The keywords will appear. Scroll through it and pick the ones you can use for your profile.

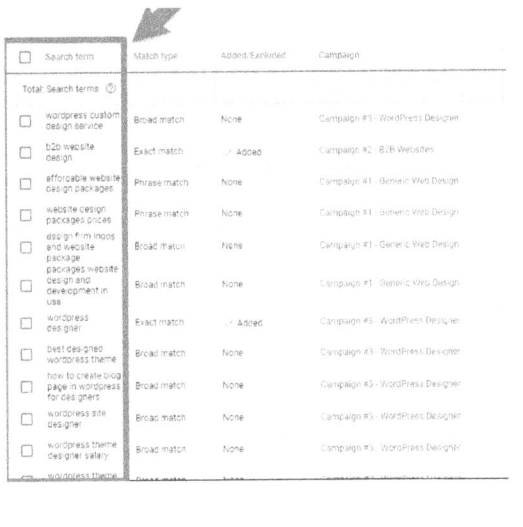

Mastering the Art of Side Hustle | Page 35

Step 3: Search on LinkedIn. Login to your LinkedIn profile and on the search area type in your industry and click Advanced. It is going to show you the words related to your industry that are most searched. You can then use these keywords to incorporate on your online profile.

C. Put Your Experience and Achievements First

Traditional resumes list tasks they have performed on their professional experience. Although that is not wrong for certain positions, it would be better if you highlight your work-related achievements if you have any. This is especially helpful for work-from-home online jobs because employers are always more concerned about the results rather than the daily process.

Academic background should be of lesser priorities unless the job you are applying for requires you to have those degrees such as teaching jobs.

Putting a career objective is not necessary but if you're going to put one, make sure that it is witty and captivating. Write it the way you would write headlines for posters and billboards, short, succinct, and most importantly, attention-grabbing.

D. K.I.S.S.

Follow the K.I.S.S. principle. Keep it short and sweet. Your sentences should be concrete descriptions of your achievements and skills and should not be embellished with unnecessary adjectives. Try typing your job descriptions on a word document first. If your sentences are filling up more than one line, consider editing it. Contrary to popular belief, using big words won't impress any hiring manager. Actual achievements will. Keep your sentences simple. Avoid compound sentences.

PDF Version Of Your Profile

Aside from your platform-based profile, you should also prepare a PDF version of your resume. This will allow you to send your profile to anyone, even to those that are outside the job sites.

However, you cannot afford to write a long PDF version of your profile. You have to prepare a condensed version. Your online profile may be filled with credentials to help the site's SEO but you don't have that benefit when sending your resume outside of the site.

Benefits of a PDF
- You can make it more creative if your industry or the job position calls for it
- You can send it to anyone because time will come when current clients will recommend you to other people who are not necessarily in that site
- You can make several versions that would fit the job you are applying to and make it more focused
- You can also use it on websites like Indeed and ZipRecruiter and other traditional job application channels

Personal Website

Two important things that people ignore are:
- Buying their own name domain
- Building their own website

Buying your name domain simply means buying [yourname].com. For example, if your name is Adelle Stafford, you should buy www.adellestafford.com. You should then build a website using that URL because once you establish yourself, people can refer you to other people. When they search your name, it would be easier to port them to a website that is directly connected to you. Doing business with you directly saves you from having to pay fees on those websites and further opens you to other opportunities.

Here are some online sites I use to buy domains and set up emails:

- namecheap.com
- squarespace.com
- wix.com

I used these sites because they make it easy to set up my email and do not force me to buy more services or products like Wordpress does.

> Hot Tip!
> You can set up your own email using your domain, don't have to pay for a server. For example:
> - You have a free email: janedoe@gmail.com
> - You bought your own domain: janedoe.com
> - You want to set up jane@janedoe.com
>
> You can forward all the emails being sent to jane@janedoe.com to janedoe@gmail.com. Just set jane@janedoe.com. This is what you call an "alias". Depending on what email service you are using and domain server from where you bought your domain set up will vary. I suggest you google the step by step process of how you can do it.

Now let's get down to the expenses that will be required when you do this:

Item	Squarespace	GoDaddy
URL	$9.99 annually	$12.99 annually
Website Hosting	From $16.99mo	$99 annually
Email	Free - $15.00 mo	$5.99 - $50.00 monthly

Note: that the pricing or URL varies but I am showing the average

You can pay someone $100 to create your website. Hire someone on Upwork. A simple one-page website is not expensive to make and does the job just fine. The advantage of using a platform like Squarespace or Wix is that it is easy to use. You don't need a lot of technical skills to be able to maintain it yourself.

However, if you are a web designer or a graphic designer or in an industry that's related to art, I will recommend that you create a more elaborate website that will showcase your talent. If, however, your profession falls under something that does not require elaborate design, a one-page website is enough.

Tips in Creating Your Own Website

It is no different from writing your own profile on the website of job sites. You need to use keywords that are most searched under or related to your own profession. Use those words as part of your job description or blog posts.

Keep it clean and direct to the point on the landing area. The landing area is the visible part that a person sees once they land on your website. If you're an accountant, it is probably not important for prospective employers to see anything elaborate in terms of design but it is very important for them to know the quality of your work within the first 3 seconds. Below is an example of a good website for an accountant.

There is nothing elaborate about the website. The website uses one professional looking photo and the rest are words but you know exactly what the professional is offering. Remember that you have, at the most, five Seconds to capture your audience, three if you're being conservative. That means that your website needs to load fast and you need to deliver the best pitch that you can about yourself. If you're an accountant for example, I would suggest that you put your best achievement or best qualification on the front page. For example if you are a lawyer-accountant specializing in startup businesses, put that on the landing area. I would also suggest you put a professional image or photo of yourself. You don't need a professional photographer to take a professional photo of yourself. All you need is good lighting and a good location.

Contact. Put a phone number and an email address and an office address. I know that a lot of you would feel uneasy about putting your own phone number, email address, and address on your website because it makes you prone to spammers and other threats. You will find below some resources you could use to make all of this possible without putting too much personal information about yourself.

Photos. You don't need a professional photographer to take professional looking photos. You can use your iPhone and use some filters. Here are some tips:

1) Sunlight should be shining on you. Although it is tempting to take a photo of yourself outside, the lighting can be tricky. Just remember that the light source should be in front of you not behind you. Avoid casting as shadow on your face and make sure your eyes are clearly visible.

Shiny and glossy areas on the skin

2) Dress nicely. A Blazer or a shirt with a collar always makes you look more professional.

3) You don't need a makeup artist especially if you're a guy but be mindful of the oily spots on your skin. Eye makeup remover pads or facial wipe will do the trick. There is an a-line on the face that is most

prone to being oily on screen. That's in the nose area. Wipe your face and pay special attention to the spot before going on camera. See image on the left.

4) Use an iPhone to take a picture of yourself. If you want to use the photo for your website, the image should be horizontal. It would be good if you have an iPhone 10 because it does have the best camera. They said that Google pixel also takes good photos but I have not tried it.

5) Some ideas on how to pose:
   a) If you have a desk at home, tidy it up and lean on it. Look at the camera and smile.
   b) You can also sit on a chair or a couch, cross your legs and smile as sweetly as you can.
   c) An action shot like you in front of a computer and working not looking at the camera will also work or you having a casual conversation with somebody.

Free Resources You Can Use for Your Website

Google Voice. Google Voice is a free app from Google that allows you to get a phone number for free and ports that phone number to your existing phone. From this app you can text people, make calls, and receive calls on the same phone that you have without your personal number being revealed.

All you need to do is create a Gmail account and then download Google Voice. You may also use Google Voice on your desktop. Just go to https://voice.google.com/. It may ask you to sign in again if you are using Google Voice for the first time. Use your newly created or old Gmail account. That Google Voice account will then be connected to your Gmail account and your phone. If you use Google Voice on your phone or desktop, you don't pay a dime.

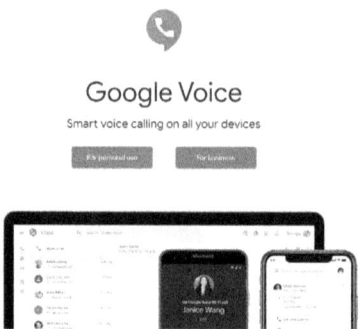

A screenshot of Google Voice Website

Email as an alias in Gmail. You may use your own domain as an email at no extra cost through Google. For example, if you just bought the website www.AccountantInSeattle.com, you may create the email admin@accountantinseattle.com. You can reply using an email you created under your new domain if you created it on Google. Just log in to your gmail and go to Settings> Accounts> Add Email. You may also call Google Domains for assistance. It's free. See instructions below.

Step 1: Login to your email.

Step 2: Click Settings (the wheel symbol on the upper right hand side)

Step 3: Click Accounts and then add another email.

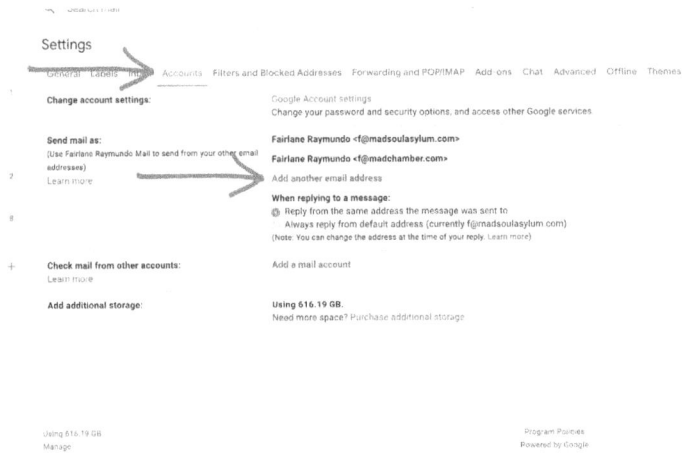

Step 4: Follow the prompts.

Business address. You can always use your own address for your business address but if you don't feel comfortable about it you can always get a PO box. There are different options: PO Box via USPS for as low as $20, mail handling services of co working spaces such as Regus and WeWork for as low as $45, or virtual offices for as little as $10 a month. The rates will highly depend on the location you choose. The prices mentioned are the lowest possible price point.

A virtual mailbox will scan your mails and send it to your selected email address. You may opt for additional perks such as forwarding the physical mail to your physical address which is useful If you're receiving credit cards or imported documents from the government.

Other Tips

- If you need to hire a resume writer, do so. You can always hire someone in one of the job sites we mentioned. The $100 investment on a resume

writer is well worth it if it will gain you employment or projects
- If you want something fancy for your website, pay someone to do it. It's not worth wasting days if not weeks for something someone can do in a day
- Start with something simple at first. Use Google services because most of them are free. You can shift to a paid one once you are set up
- Offer free consultation on your website

Step 2: Writing an Effective Resume or Portfolio

Now that we know the basics of creating your own websites and creating your own profile, let's get down to the difficult part. How do you actually create a profile or a professional website that will convince employers to hire you?

I am going to introduce to you a term that is most widely used in the advertising and marketing industry. The unique selling proposition.

The Unique Selling Proposition

The unique selling proposition or USP simply means the one thing that you offer that other people do not. This might be difficult to crack especially if you think that you are just another ordinary employee. So the first step is to believe that there is something that you offer that others do not or only a few offers. The next step is for you to know what that is.

Also remember that although it is possible, it would be very difficult for you to become the one unique person that possesses something others don't but it is very likely that you have something that very few people offer.

For example, an accountant lawyer is rare. It is even rarer to find somebody with a strong online presence.

If you are a chemical engineer, you could have worked for an important project where you were a part of the engineering team.

If you are a fashion designer and you've had experience doing sublimation prints or direct to fabric printing, it's rare for other designers to also have technical skills.

If you are a veterinarian, you may have had experience doing animal training with kids.

If you are a paralegal, you may have had experience doing more work than an ordinary paralegal does including writing deposition and proof ups.

If you are an online customer service support representative, you may have had experience handling both technology- and media-related companies.

For Fresh Graduates

You don't need experience to have a USP. It can also be a unique skill combination, not necessarily experience. Do you have a rare combination of skills? Do you speak multiple languages? Do you know multiple software languages?

Are you a part of the campaign or project that made it big and hit the mainstream media?

Do you know both coding and writing?

Do you have access to resources others don't, such as Nielsen research?

Once you find your USP, use that as your career highlight or you can do the way that I do it, I actually call it my unique selling proposition. That's the first thing on my portfolio.

Presenting Your Professional Experience Properly

After your career highlight or USP, put your professional experience.

I always put the name of the company first, then my job title. If you have been doing freelance work the rule still applies.

Incorporate your achievements with your job description. See examples below:

✗	✓
managed all social media accounts from content plan	increased social media following from 1,000 to 30,000 in a span of six months through

to content creation to scheduling to monitoring	unique and relevant content planning and creation, continuous strategy evaluation, monitoring of industry trends, and working with marketers and partners with a limited budget
10-year experience as a pre-school teacher	created an after-school program that helped students make professional connections and raise funds for the school's after school programs
12-year sales experience	developed a research strategy and international network that resulted to the expansion of client's market to 10 different states and sales growth of 500% as a direct result of customer service

For Fresh Graduates or Those With No Achievement

The next question is what if you do not have any achievement but you do know that you do your work efficiently and diligently. Simply skip the achievements part but make your job description as concrete as possible. See examples below:

✘	✔
customer service representative and receptionist	Implemented a detailed guest management system to ensure no guest or phone call waits for more than 3 minutes without a response
game programmer specializing in character creation	worked on character creation of online games

	such as game A, game B or game C
12-year sales experience	developed a research strategy and international network that resulted 2 the expansion of clients Market the 10 different states and sales growth 500% as a direct result of customer service

Resume Examples

A good example of a creative resume.

DWAYNE CARTER

123 State Street, Stamford, CT · (203) 555-5555 · carter@dwayne.com

NOT-FOR-PROFIT EXECUTIVE

– Public Relations/Marketing/Fundraising/Administration/Grant Writing –

Accomplished fundraiser combining entrepreneurial spirit with an ability to draw leaders from business, government and not-for-profit together in a common cause

Over 10 years executive management experience including non-profit, private business and state and local government. Proven track record of building partnerships and coalitions among business, government and non-profit organizations. Hands-on entrepreneur who has also led organizations of up to 750. Special Expertise includes:

- Coalition and Partnership Building
- Sales Presentations/Public Speaking
- New Business Development
- Media Campaign Orchestration
- P&L and Budget Management
- Team Building and Leadership

SELECTED CAREER HIGHLIGHTS

- **As Special Assistant for the Governor of Connecticut:** Led successful fundraising campaign for the "New Start" program, obtaining 30% of funding from business.
- **As Founder and President of Compro:** Built multi-million dollar PR and Marketing agency within five years.
- **As Senior Associate at Sandler Communications:** Designed and led awareness-raising campaign for the Wellness Initiative, which aimed to reduce malnutrition. Built strong coalition of industry associations, government agencies and unions.
- **As Volunteer:** Developed communication and fundraising strategies for small non-profit clients.

PROFESSIONAL HISTORY

COMPRO COMMUNICATIONS   1999 – Present
Multi-million dollar PR and advertising agency servicing a variety of clients nationwide – Stamford CT

Founder & President

Founded agency to work with Fortune 500 clients, non-profits and political issue campaigns. Lead team of PR/marketing professionals on client acquisition, business strategy, staffing, financial management and operations. Partnered with New York Public Relations on a variety of client projects.

- Created partnership between Compro and the state government to retrieve federal Medicare refunds which has raised $100M to date.
- Provided pro-bono PR and fundraising help to non-profits including New York Hospice Organization and the Forest Hills School in Queens, which helps children with special needs.
- Managed campaign for New Jersey Education Lottery which passed in 2002 and has generated more than $250M per year for education.

Observe how his achievements are highlighted and come before the Professional history.

Step 3: Applying for Jobs or Bidding for Projects

First Goal: Accumulate reviews

Your most immediate goal is to accumulate reviews because this will establish your reputation on that job site. Reviews is one of the first things an employer will check once you apply for a job or bid for a project. Ten is the ideal number. If you get 10 reviews, it will be easier for future employers to trust you.

How to Secure Jobs ASAP

Bid low. I was charging $1.50 per 100 hundred words on writing assignments when I was starting. I know that this is extremely low for U.S. standards but I wanted and needed to establish my reputation quickly. I decided to bid low just to get the ball rolling.

If you are a native english speaker located in North America, it would even be more of an advantage for you because most employers are located in the West. They are always looking for native english speakers or providers that are located in the same country as they are for easier communication. If you bid low and are in the same country as the employer, it would even be easier for you to get projects.

Go for Project-Based Jobs. I sought out project-based jobs in the beginning because those requirements hire faster. These are projects where I wasn't paid until the project is concluded. This has since changed. Nowadays, you can set milestones so that you get paid after the completion of certain stages of the job. Many freelancers still don't like this, preferring per-hour jobs. However, project based jobs usually have fast turn around. I got them done quickly and asked for a review as soon as it was done.

Low Pay for Reviews. There are also a lot of employers that would openly offer lower pay in exchange for good reviews. Some people feel that this is abuse but I simply look at it as an investment. If I can get those 10 good reviews as fast as I can then the sooner I can charge the rate that I actually deserve. And that's what I did. I was careful to look at the employer's review though. If they have done a lot of transactions in the past and have good feedback from employees, then I sign up.

For about 15 projects I was getting paid $1.50 for 100 words for the articles that I was writing. For a 1500-word article I was getting paid $15. Anybody in the Philippines will tell you that $15 is not bad considering, at the time, minimum wage was $2 an hour. However, that's not acceptable here in the US. I knew that but it was more important for me to establish myself as fast as I could. After the first six months, I slowly started getting my rate up to the level that I think I deserve. By the third year I already had a full-time job that was paying me $15 an hour and I was still in the Philippines and regular online jobs that were paying me $10 an hour.

Write a Professional Application Letter or Proposal

I already had a ready-made application letter depending on the job and industry to which I was applying. I would make adjustments, primarily by incorporating keywords found on the job post into my resume or profile. I had an application letter for writing jobs on travel sites, a separate application letter for writing jobs for financial sites, a separate application letter for social media planning, and others.

Include Keywords Found in the Job Post

A big adjustment that I make on my resume and application letter is the use of keywords. I would usually revise my application letter and resume to include terminologies that the employer used in its job post.

For example, in my standard resume, I do not usually include my experience in writing speeches for the President. However, if the job I am applying for requires that I write speeches or that I have experience in political commentary, then I include that.

Read the Whole Description

Many employers actually include instructions within the job descriptions that are easily ignored. You need to make sure to read the entire job description to catch those instructions.

For example, I would personally put the instruction to use "Optimus Prime" as the subject of their email in the middle of the job description that I posted. Everyone who doesn't follow that instruction is automatically dropped. It demonstrates the applicant's ability to follow instructions and it is a gauge on how serious the applicant is on my job post.

Include a Freebie

I usually include a freebie, usually a 10 + 1. That means for every 10 articles that they ask me to write I will give them one free. Eventually, when I created my own business (more on that later), I started offering additional services that I hope to "sell". For example, if I am working as a customer service representative for a client, I can offer free five hours research or free writing of one blog post. It will serve two purposes. It is my USP, one that I know other providers won't offer. More importantly, it is a form of cross-selling. By giving them a taste of what else I can offer, I am enhancing my value as a provider and it gives me a chance to have an additional source of income by providing more services to an existing market. .

Include Samples of Work

Always include your portfolio.

A portfolio isn't just for artists, writers or other creative professions. Every professional should have a portfolio, whether it's a list of clients you've handled before, projects you've managed or worked for, or publications under your name.

It is advisable to have different types of portfolio for different industries to which you are applying, one that is customized to the job you are trying to secure. If you are trying to secure a customer service job for a tech product, then prepare a portfolio that shows your experience working on tech products. If you are applying to a non-profit company, list down the non-profit projects or companies in which you worked.

Your Online Visibility

The LinkedIn Key

LinkedIn is the most popular site for professionals because it has credibility and visibility. When people search for names of a specific person, LinkedIn is one of the top websites that Google pulls from. More importantly, accounts are verifiable which raises the level of authenticity.

Make sure you complete your LinkedIn profile the way you would your online profile on the job sites. Make sure it is detailed, complete and has an accompanying portfolio. Also, make sure to put a professional-looking photo.

Keep Yourself Open to New Opportunities

On LinkedIn, there is an option for you to let employers and Headhunters know that you are open to opportunities. I just keep that open all the time even when I'm not looking. If there is something good enough for me to leave my current job, then I will do it. I have been approached by several Headhunters and some of them have already resulted in interviews. Some prospects are good but none of it has yielded something good enough for me to leave my current job. Do note that when I say better it doesn't only mean better in terms of finances. I am pursuing other things that require time. The job that I have right now allows me to work from home several days a week. That means I cut on travel time. I use that time to pursue other things, specifically my writing and my YouTube channel.

Connect With Headhunters

Start with Headhunters. Send them your profile, websites, resume, portfolio, and a professionally written introduction letter. Headhunters will never turn down a resume. They need that. And they will always have you as a candidate if something related to your qualifications comes up.

Add headhunters to your network so you are directly related to them. Gaining direct links to as many people as you can will allow you to be closer to other people that might be able to give you better opportunities. For example, if a Headhunter that you are directly connected with is directly connected to somebody from Google or Amazon or Nestle or a company for which you want to work for, then you are one connection away from those people. More importantly these people are most likely the ones that have to get you an interview with their companies.

Upload Relevant Content

Remember that the key is recognition and connection. When you are recognizable and credible, it is easier for you to find the right connection. Be active on LinkedIn:

1) Join credible groups within LinkedIn and actually participate in discussions
2) Regularly put contents on your own page and on group pages
3) Connect with as many people as you can related to your industry
4) When someone reaches out to you and sends you a message, reply even though it is just to politely thank them for reaching out or just to acknowledge their message.
5) Make sure that you post relevant contents. For example, instead of just posting photos of you working which you also must do, you also need to make sure that the photos reflect a certain achievement or activity related to your job like an inauguration of a

project that you managed or opening of a coffee shop that you designed and helped build. Make every post count.

Tag People

Tag people related to the projects or work that you are doing.

Being able to connect with others, especially if they are already established in your own industry, is going to add to your credibility, visibility, and employability. The wider your network, the bigger your chances of getting connected to someone that could employ you.

So make sure to reach out to as many people as you can. Say hi to them, congratulate them on their work anniversaries, and achievements.

Help Others

If there is somebody who asks for your help in following a page or liking an article that they posted, do it.

Go the extra mile and leave a comment too. It's free and it's not going to take any more than five seconds of your time. When it's your turn to ask for help, go back to these people and ask for help. Most likely only 10% will return the favor. But this is a game of numbers. Getting back 10% of the help that you extended to them is better than not getting any at all.

Leave Digital Footprints

Digital Footprints mean that you make yourself searchable and visible online strong enough so that when people search for you or for services you offer or qualifications that you possess, you will be visible or that you will show up on their search result.

There are different ways of doing it. The most obvious of which is social media because that's free and easy to create. But there are other ways that you can be digital footprints that is less known but is nonetheless important:

- Ebooks
- YouTube Portfolio

- Forums
- Free or paid PR
- Websites specializing on your industry

Let's go through it one by one.

Social Media

Post photos of past recognition or projects. It would be better if you can accompany it with a description that mentions what the project is for and what it has achieved.

To add credibility, tag people involved in the project and official company social media page. This will erase doubts that you were simply a spectator in the event.

Make sure to use relevant hashtags as well. This is going to allow people to see your posts that are not following you or liking you.

Ebooks

Ebooks or white papers are great ways to establish your credibility. It doesn't have to be published by a big publishing company. You can self publish it and put it out on Amazon for sale or other publishing platforms. You may also make it available as a free download. The point is to get something out there that is professionally written and is substantial to represent you.

An Ebook should be professionally written. It has to follow an academic format either an APA or Chicago. I know it sounds daunting but even I can't format an Ebook without an APA guide or Chicago guidebook. The good news is that there are plenty of guides online that you can access for free. See the Free Resources section.

If you are not particularly a writer it would be advisable to just create an outline and ask somebody else to ghost write for you. Again, it doesn't have to be expensive; you can always tap Freelancers through upwork and other job sites. Don't forget to ask the freelancer to sign a Non Disclosure Agreement.

Also, the basic content should come from you. A resume writer will enhance your resume but not make up things for you.

YouTube Portfolio

You can create a video portfolio on YouTube. If you don't know how to do this, just hire somebody that will write and conceptualize your portfolio. This is a new way to present yourself.

This is relevant even if the industry you are in isn't necessarily related to entertainment. People are generally more akin to watching rather than reading. Even if you're a veterinarian, biologist, researcher, accountant, or customer service representative, you can always have an attractive video portfolio. It doesn't have to be long but it has to be well presented to speak about your credentials.

Just look at it this way, this is a video version of your resume.

You can get a writer for as low as $50 on upwork and then editor for as low as $50 also on upwork. They are most likely not people that are located in the United States but there are certain countries, like the Philippines, that speak English well enough to be able to write a good script for your video.

Join Forums

Some professions have established forums. You can create an account and participate in the discussion but don't just post useless facts. Be helpful. When people are asking questions and you know the answer, provide it. This is going to let your name be known to other people within the industry. And this can lead to recommendations to other prospective employers.

If you don't know any good forum, Google is always a good place to start. Just type in your industry name and the word forums and hit Search. Go to the websites and start creating accounts. After several days of observations, you'd determine which forums are actually good. Groups within social media such as Facebook groups or LinkedIn groups would also be a good way for you to participate in discussion and get your name out to other people within your industry.

Specialized Websites

Make sure you have a profile on websites specializing in your industry. For example, if you are involved in making movies, TV shows or books, the International Movie Database (IMDB) is a good source of information. Make sure that your name is mentioned in the movies or TV shows that you have participated in.

PR

PR stands for a public relations or press release. You can get free PR by creating accounts on free PR sites.

Check the Resources section for links to free PR sites that I use and have proven to be credible and gold VR sites.

PR is news. The release has to be written like the news. Therefore the content should be newsworthy.

If you have a new white paper or ebook out, that's news. It should follow the 4W format. Meaning, the first part should immediately answer the what, who, when, and where questions followed by the why and then the how.

If you can afford it, you can pay for PR which gives you more exposure but is expensive.

You can also utilize paid content sharing like Outbrain. They are websites that provide content to other established magazines or newspapers. It is paid but it is cheaper than a PR. Also, you can set your own budget as to how much you want to spend.

More Tips 💡

Tips on Commissioning Ghost Writers

Make sure to have your NDA ready. ready this ebook is going to include the usual NBA that I provide contract workers that I hire. Go through it and then you can revise it accordingly.

If you are very lazy to write like I am, Google Voice Typing is another good way to do it. Just go into Google Docs, click Tools and choose Voice Typing. All you have to do is make sure that you have a good microphone or an earpiece with the mic.

Dictate it and Google Docs will actually transcribe that into a text. It is not going to be perfect, especially if you have an accent but for Native Americans it would be 95% accurate. The only manual thing that you will need to do will be the formatting.

You can also simply record the contents and have the person who's writing the ebook transcribe it for you.

Rewriting was a common practice 10 years ago. That means people will simply get a book or an established ebook and then have somebody reword the entire thing. That way, they will not be accused of plagiarizing. This is not advisable anymore because online or Ebooks have become very popular sources of information, it is much easier for people to get their hands on the original ideas. Being a copy of somebody else isn't going to establish your name or make you benefit from it.

You can utilize free online PR to get the word out about your ebook. I am going to discuss this in detail below. You can also use LinkedIn and other social media sites. You can allow people to download your ebook for free. If your goal is to simply leave digital Footprints rather than earn from it.

A good length of an ebook really depends on the content. If it is instructional and your topic is very focused, 10 pages including pictures and sources would be enough. If it is a white paper or something that is more academic in nature, something as short as five pages if your topic is very focused.

However covering something that is wider in terms of coverage of the topic would require longer

> ones. Again if your goal is to simply leave digital footprints then you don't need something long as long as the content is good.

Directly Email Headhunters and Decision Makers

I also send my portfolio and resume to Headhunters and decision-makers of different companies even if they are not looking for hiring somebody like me. Getting a job is just a game of numbers - more applications equals more chances of getting work.

This tactic I have been using for the past 15 years and it has yielded to only three projects. However, those projects were significant to my experience and two continue to work with me to this day on special projects.

Although 15 years of doing something with only 3 projects as a direct result may seem like nothing, the exponential result says otherwise. Besides, it only takes me an hour every month to do it. There are months I would skip it, especially when I am busy with other projects.

You can find headhunters and decision makers of companies on LinkedIn and by searching for them on Google. Sometimes, I would search randomly. I'd think of a company that interests me and search for the decision makers on LinkedIn or Google. Sometimes, I pick clues from job posts. If Adidas posted a job vacancy in the Research department, then I search for the decision maker's name for Adidad on Google or LinkedIn.

Most of the emails I send go unanswered.

Step 4: Grow

Branch out and set up a company

The most significant change in my life as a Freelance life is my migration to the U.S. I knew that freelancers based in the U.S. got more opportunities so I established my own company in the US and registered myself as a company or service provider in Upwork. I hired other people from other countries and bidded for more projects. I passed on the work to my team and took a referral or management fee. This is no different from setting up an actual company. Where you get the projects and you have people hiring for you.

I always make sure that the person that I'm working with would know that I actually have a company and that I will not be doing the project all by myself. If the employer demands that I directly do the job I usually charge higher. Because I'm going to have to give up other things to be able to do the job that he is requiring.

Do not rush to get to this point. It's going to take several years of establishing yourself to be able to get to this point but once you do, it is no different from having your own company.

Hire people from different parts of Asia where the minimum wage is lower. I submitted a bid with a regular US wage standard. This still allowed me to pay my freelancers higher than their country's wage standards.

Scout for Clients on Social Media

I also scout for clients on social media. LinkedIn is a very good source. I have an online company profile that I give and send to prospective clients. Startups are always good because my rate is not as high as bigger companies but I provide end to end services. I also don't tie them to a contract. We go project per project or month to month.

Challenge Encountered

Starting Out

Getting the first client is a challenge. Getting the second client is even more of a challenge. The competition is stiff and if you are in the US, you are competing against Asians who can pull down the prices low to the 10th of US minimum wage and still be paid well enough. I was still in the Philippines when I started. I also had a full-time job. That gave me an advantage in terms of bid price. I was also not "desperate" to get projects because I had a full time job.

It was a matter of making sacrifices just to get my feet wet. I pulled my price low and took more risks.

Clients Not Paying

I had at least three clients, that I remember, who didn't pay me. I gave them a bad review on UpWork but they simply deleted their account. It was frustrating but I chose to look at it in terms of percentage. Three unpaid jobs compared to the hundreds I got isn't bad. Every job has a risk. This is the one that comes with being an online freelancer.

This may happen to you too. I wish it won't but it can. Take all the precautions such as checking employer reputation, avoiding per project jobs, and keeping all communications within the job sites. However, do know that despite all these precautions, it may still happen.

Time Zones

I was in the Philippines when I started online freelance work but most clients are coming from the U.S., Europe and Australia. I am always half a day ahead. Naturally, I had to make the adjustment. I had to stay up late so I could communicate with them.

I didn't have to stay up all the hours but I still had to make sure I overlap with their work hours significantly. It limited the jobs I could take when I still had a full time job but got better when I started doing online freelance work full time.

Internet Speed

The Philippines has one of the worst internet connection speeds in the world. It was a constant struggle to try and communicate with employers in the U.S. Employers understood the nature of the internet in the Philippines but there were times when it still got to them.

That won't be a problem if you are in the U.S. or in countries with fast internet connection.

Useful Resources

For Editing PDF Documents: PDFPro.com

I find myself having to edit PDF documents more often than I care. Getting Acrobat Pro is expensive. PDF Pro is a much cheaper way to be able to edit PDF documents. If you settle for a free account, you can edit up to three documents daily. If you opt for a paid account, for $50 a year, you can edit an unlimited amount of documents.

Acrobat Pro is $12.99 a month. There are other apps that do the same function but none as cheap as PDFPro.com.

Google Suite

Google Suite is a good source for a lot of things: replacement for Microsoft Office, Cloud Storage, Business phone, Website Hosting, and others, all for free. Do remember that profitability is important to me. I always look for ways to milk my investments for all its worth. So, if I can get something for free, I don't pay.

To access everything Google Suite offers, all you need is a free gmail account.

Microsoft Word and Excel Replacement: Google Docs

I don't have Microsoft Word anymore because I don't want to pay the annual fee. I use Google Docs. It allows me to read and edit Word Documents. Once I am done and I need to send it to someone, I just explored it as a Word document and send it.

It also has the ability to take voice dictation and convert my voice recording into text. In fact this is how I am writing this ebook completely. It is not perfect and I still do some editing but I am able to "write" even when I am lying down on bed, stuck in traffic, or doing my daily walk.

Business Phone Number and Messaging: Google Voice

It also allows me to store all of my documents without having to fear losing my USB. It also has Google Voice which allows me to have my own business phone number and use it on my own phone so that I can call and respond to people without disclosing my personal phone number.

Domain Buying: Google Domains

I buy all of my domains on Google domains because it allows me to create free emails and it also allows me to protect my own data or personal information at no additional cost. If I buy my domain and want to keep my identity private on GoDaddy, I need to pay an extra $15. It's free on Google Domains.

I can also get a professional email service for free on Google Domains. It is at least $1.99 monthly on GoDaddy but that comes with a lot of conditions.

Social Media Management: Hootsuite

HootSuite is a platform that allows me to schedule my social media posts ahead of time. I have a free account which only allows me to connect three social media accounts of up to 30 contents. If you have the budget, you can actually pre-post unlimited number of posts and connect unlimited number of social media sites.

There are other social media management platforms but none provides the amount of service Hootsuite does on their free tier.

Project Management
- Trello
- Asana

I often use Trello. Simply because I like the layout and I don't necessarily want so much details about projects. All I need is to be able to be reminded of the projects that I have existing and projects that are pending. Every morning I open my Trello and check what are the things that need to be done and things that have been pending for quite some time.

Asana also has a free tier and if you are the kind that wants a lot of details in their project management platform, Asana is for you.

Writing Guides

If you need to write an academic paper, here are some free resources:

- APA Guidebook: https://owl.purdue.edu/owl/research_and_citation/apa_style/apa_formatting_and_style_guide/reference_list_books.html
- Chicago Guidebook: https://owl.purdue.edu/owl/research_and_citation/chicago_manual_17th_edition/cmos_formatting_and_style_guide/chicago_manual_of_style_17th_edition.html

Free PR Sites

- PRLog.com
- PRBUzz.com
- ClickPress.com
- I-Newswire.com

NON-DISCLOSURE AGREEMENT (NDA) Sample

This Nondisclosure Agreement (the "Agreement") is entered into by and between _____ with its principal offices at _____, ("Disclosing Party") and _____, located at _____ ("Receiving Party") for the purpose of preventing the unauthorized disclosure of Confidential Information as defined below. The parties agree to enter into a confidential relationship concerning the disclosure of certain proprietary and confidential information ("Confidential Information").

1. **Definition of Confidential Information**. For purposes of this Agreement, "Confidential Information" shall include all information or material that has or could have commercial value or other utility in the business in which Disclosing Party is engaged. If Confidential Information is in written form, the Disclosing Party shall label or stamp the materials with the word "Confidential" or some similar warning. If Confidential Information is transmitted

orally, the Disclosing Party shall promptly provide writing indicating that such oral communication constituted Confidential Information.

    2. **Exclusions from Confidential Information**. Receiving Party's obligations under this Agreement do not extend to information that is: (a) publicly known at the time of disclosure or subsequently becomes publicly known through no fault of the Receiving Party; (b) discovered or created by the Receiving Party before disclosure by Disclosing Party; (c) learned by the Receiving Party through legitimate means other than from the Disclosing Party or Disclosing Party's representatives; or (d) is disclosed by Receiving Party with Disclosing Party's prior written approval.

    3. **Obligations of Receiving Party**. Receiving Party shall hold and maintain the Confidential Information in strictest confidence for the sole and exclusive benefit of the Disclosing Party. Receiving Party shall carefully restrict access to Confidential Information to employees, contractors and third parties as is reasonably required and shall require those persons to sign nondisclosure restrictions at least as protective as those in this Agreement. Receiving Party shall not, without the prior written approval of Disclosing Party, use for Receiving Party's benefit, publish, copy, or otherwise disclose to others, or permit the use by others for their benefit or to the detriment of Disclosing Party, any Confidential Information. Receiving Party shall return to Disclosing Party any and all records, notes, and other written, printed, or tangible materials in its possession pertaining to Confidential Information immediately if Disclosing Party requests it in writing.

    4. **Time Periods**. The nondisclosure provisions of this Agreement shall survive the termination of this Agreement and Receiving Party's duty to hold Confidential Information in confidence shall remain in effect until the Confidential Information no longer qualifies as a trade secret or until Disclosing Party sends Receiving Party written notice releasing Receiving Party from this Agreement, whichever occurs first.

5. **Relationships**. Nothing contained in this Agreement shall be deemed to constitute either party a partner, joint venture or employee of the other party for any purpose.

6. **Severability**. If a court finds any provision of this Agreement invalid or unenforceable, the remainder of this Agreement shall be interpreted so as best to affect the intent of the parties.

7. **Integration**. This Agreement expresses the complete understanding of the parties with respect to the subject matter and supersedes all prior proposals, agreements, representations, and understandings. This Agreement may not be amended except in writing signed by both parties.

8. **Waiver**. The failure to exercise any right provided in this Agreement shall not be a waiver of prior or subsequent rights.

9. **Notice of Immunity**. Employee is provided notice that an individual shall not be held criminally or civilly liable under any federal or state trade secret law for the disclosure of a trade secret that is made (i) in confidence to a federal, state, or local government official, either directly or indirectly, or to an attorney; and (ii) solely for the purpose of reporting or investigating a suspected violation of law; or is made in a complaint or other document filed in a lawsuit or other proceeding, if such filing is made under seal. An individual who files a lawsuit for retaliation by an employer for reporting a suspected violation of law may disclose the trade secret to the attorney of the individual and use the trade secret information in the court proceeding, if the individual (i) files any document containing the trade secret under seal; and (ii) does not disclose the trade secret, except pursuant to court order.

This Agreement and each party's obligations shall be binding on the representatives, assigns and successors of such party. Each party has signed this Agreement through its authorized representative.

DISCLOSING PARTY

Signature _____

Typed or Printed Name _____

Date: _____

RECEIVING PARTY

Signature _____

Typed or Printed Name _____

Date: _____

Checklist

Reading this ebook and watching the video is only the first step. The more important part is actually being able to implement everything on this ebook or video.

Below is a checklist that will serve a guide on the things that you need to do to ensure that you're following every step of the way.

1. Resume
   a. 1-page version
   b. Extensive version
2. Government-issued IDs for verification
3. Portfolio
4. Professionally-written application letter
5. URL of your own name and your industry
6. Links to works you have published or articles written about you
7. A "for public consumption" version of your Social Media Accounts
8. Check and sign up on the following online job sites:

      a. Upwork.com

      b. Freelancer.com

      c. Guru.com

      d. Academia-Research.com

9. LinkedIn Account Set up

www.ingramcontent.com/pod-product-compliance
Lightning Source LLC
Chambersburg PA
CBHW071943210526
45479CB00002B/800